Mutual Trespasses

Dear Jim and Beverly —

To someone (s)
who "adds
grace to the
world."

Phil

MUTUAL TRESPASSES

Philip Fried

Ion Books/*Raccoon*
3387 Poplar Ave., Suite 205
Memphis, TN 38111

Ion Books/*Raccoon*
3387 Poplar Avenue, Suite 205
Memphis, TN 38111

A *Raccoon* Book

Library of Congress Cataloging-in-Publication Data

Fried, Philip, 1945-

  Mutual trespasses.

  I. Title.
PS3556.R48828M881988811'.5487-26287
ISBN 0-938507-13-3
ISBN 0-938507-12-5 (pbk.)

Cover: *Disks of Newton - Study for Fugue* by Frank Kupka.
Philadelphia Museum of Art: The Louise and Walter
Arensberg Collection.

Book design by David Spicer & Diana Taylor

ACKNOWLEDGMENTS

Certain of these poems have previously appeared or will soon appear in magazines. Grateful acknowledgments are due to the following:

Beloit Poetry Journal: "Old Man among Old Men" and "Fragment of a Heretical Testament"
Chicago Review: " 'The hanged teddy bear . . .' "
Confrontation: "Measured Slices"
Connecticut Poetry Review: "Contemporary Prayer" and "When grandma died in God's dream"
Crab Creek Review: "The Kite"
Descant: "I Was Carrying Pieces of the World"
The Magazine of Speculative Poetry: "God Contemplates My Grandmother Snoring," " 'God has infinite power of change ,' " "God's Shame," and "No Plea"
Massachusetts Review: "Testament"
The Paris Review: "Seeing He Was a Museum"
Poet Lore: "The Good Book" and "Syndrome"
Poetry Northwest: "In a Barbershop"
Raccoon: "On Genesis"
Saint Andrews Review: "Grandma's Victorian Parlor," "Lethal," and "Sunday"

"Testament" was reprinted from *The Massachusetts Review,* c. 1984. The Massachusetts Review, Inc.

For my mother, father, sister, and Lynn

CONTENTS

IV

I

Testament

I am still buried
in the rich blue loam of heaven
miles deep in the sky listening
to chants of ozone,
tickled and singed by cosmic
rays whizzing by infinitesimally
close, fragmented, my delicate
wrist buried far above the expansive unruly clouds

but I want a reverse
funeral, a gathering and downward
march, a cortege to the chorus
of every voice in the universe
that faithfully repeats, from human
prayers for safety to the chemical
whispered shuttling of genes
that freight themselves, with hardly

a loss, down the generations,
but let them halt my procession
every second, as in the funeral
pomps of African chiefs, crying boastful
laments: "How can we let you fall
from this great death lower than the sky-
tracks of birds
and crisscross aerials,"

and I want a service that celebrates
each uncontrolled random
diversion, exception, and fall-
ency to ironclad law and as the final
act of piety let them dress
me in dungarees and lower
me by clothesline to a city corner,
anonymous and whistling.

God Contemplating the World

God contemplating the world declared,
"This is a mismatch, although most
of those many little beings believe
in me uniquely, granting me varied
forms, I for one am a henotheist.
How lonely it would be to have
only four billion men as friends
whose doings are a nano-pinprick.
Am I an only child, did I kill
or frighten away the deities
of earth, the faces diving back
into the flower's anther, the bark,
the fault and fold of rock, so rain
became rain and light only light?
I would plunge after them down the stem
flowing bravely in the xylem,
insinuate myself in the crystal
of sugar to hound the insect god
out of his lace fanatic wings,
the rabid bat-gods out of the sonar
blips, conjure the ironic snake
divinities from their ancient dryness.
I am lonely and mismatched with man,
in whom I cannot completely believe."

I Was Carrying Pieces of the World

I was carrying pieces of the world-
before-the-flood in my pockets,
plastic fragments of monsters,
ribs of whales and skulls of behemoths,
and unnamable creatures that became toys,
lurid red and garish yellow and green
bits of the ancient terror. I was an ad
hoc museum of the world before Noah.

I was searching for the book that explained
how to assemble all the childhood
models that bedevilled me and were meant
to sail, speed, or fly with such grace.
Why was there always an extra piece
at the end when the smell of glue
was rife and the finished thing rickety?
I was searching for the helpful blueprint.

I was looking for the arterial maps
that pulsed more wildly than traffic,
the roads my desire travelled from town
to city, the system with no final
goal but its own circulation,
leading me on a wild goose chase
for the false and plausible places of stories,
while the maps were bleeding into my veins.

Lift-off

God said, "I am a rocket set for blastoff,
loaded down with human paraphernalia,
the jewels they offered me over millennia,
the slaughtered creatures and tithe of the good harvest,
locks of hair, nail clippings, intimate things,
and heaviest of all the secret wishes,
invocations undisclosed to the self —
all this awaits the fiery ignition,
the final act of human imagination
in its saga of divinity: to forget,
as the mass of all they longed for shears through the clouds
and bears outward, the greatest time capsule
ever assembled. How relieved I will be to nearly
win my own authority and cease
being a figment of human imagination,
I will almost constitute a civilization
in myself — who knows, these things may breed,
stranger events have happened, the bloodied oxen
with the pullulating bacteria of wishes,
who knows what I will be when I am found,
with a small map etched in gold of this galaxy,
by then well lost, and a few garbled recordings
of harvest festivals. And what of men
in the blind past on the sapphire seed of planet . . ."

God's Fear

God said, "I am most afraid of 'middle
ground,' the time of creation when no one,
not even I, knows what will happen.
That is why I mocked up the world
in six days and rested thanking
I don't know what that it was over.
Not too badly done, inspired
some would say — take the goshawk,
I don't know what got into me —
but all the time I was filled with fear,
winging it, no wonder I made
so many claws. Things in me
were at each other, and needed a place
outside. But now I am purged and clear,
kingly, above the fray, ready
to receive prayer and act for the world's
good so far as possible,
why do I feel like praying to you?"

"When I spy into the world . . ."

When I spy into the world like a slit-
open bowel and see the worms
slithing on earth to escape the rains,
the spineless, many-tentacled hydra,
and those almost nameless creatures neither
living nor dead, the viruses,
I remember these are mirrors of me
and shrink away. I hardly knew
myself during the six days' fever.
They say I am God but I only presided
like a figurehead at the creation.
What metameric appetite
in a shovelful of muddy sand
saw its chance in that brief shambles,
convulsing itself to become a phylum?
I knew it as a total lack
of control, a loss of myself to something
greater, for the real God is not
the all-knowing, attentive Father
but the spineless, infinite-fingered whorl.

God Looks Down at the Trenches

Masks, masks, the long slit a smile
for miles . . . the white plumes on Eskimo
masks, the dangling talismans
circled round the rim are nothing
to the slash of bayonet, the barbed-
wire, mortars, scraps and heaps of metal,
not to mention flesh, in no-
man's land . . . scouring the landscape,
which stares up at me blankly,
abstracted, together the enemies
carve this one tribal mask
out of the ground, teeming workers
with little stings, sacrificing
themselves to make this glare at God.
The whole earth shall be this beholding,
a fat mask in the void, tended
by infinite, infinitesimal anthills,
solicitous for the least grain
and bevel of the blank and angry
stare which shall empty itself of living
things after it is carefully groomed,
festooned with killed forests. They
don't believe in me, believe
in carving such a face that will gaze,
minus them, out at the void, confidently.

This Ticking Thing

God said, "The amazing thing about the world
is that everything that happens happens once
and for all, and while I created it that way,
I never considered the effect of time
on me. I feel I have made a solemn toy
that holds me to its rhythm, draws me out
thinner than a sheet of beaten gold,
pervious to every particle.
For the first time in my actuality,
I witness, excluded by this functioning crystal
called the universe, and my total account
held near its clear walls is totally useless.
Even if they knew, they would deny
its truth, for they are worshippers of the way
it happens. In making time, I have made another
medium, which I do not comprehend,
and I must go to school to the grasshopper,
man, who moves through his oblivious green
savanna. The weather of eternity
is nothing, or everything, but this ticking thing
I have placed upon my firmament's cool mantel
breeds such a congeries of joy and pathos."

God's Shame

"They don't understand how backward
conditions are," God shouted
against the wind blowing
from his artificial weather
machine. "Technology
is practically in its infancy
here and no help for it —"
again his words were sucked
by air, I could barely see
his leviathan bulk, obscured
in the explosion of cotton
wads the angels had flung
against the fan to simulate
snow. "Heaven's a frontier,
this isn't appreciated
down there, the news from earth
reaches us over black
prairies, fragmented, events
are stale or unintelligible
by the time we hear, and nothing
operates properly. Look —"
he gestured at teams of putti
workmen swarming over
the ramshackle contraption
designed to produce weather
in the millennial blank.

"I wanted to manufacture
a paltry iota of change,
just think how men are gifted
with this factor, but the effort
required to whip up a puff
of wind is unthinkable.
Men are racing ahead
with lasers, holograms,
while we wrestle with bicycles —"
Here he seemed to sink
into himself, a collapsing
mountain. "Tell them how
ashamed I am what I am!"

II

The Good Book

God said, "My finger sticks
to the dictionary, its pages
are smeared with honey, and I
am a bear for words, including
'God,' who I read is 'a being
. . . the perfect omnipotent
originator and ruler
of the universe.' No picture
but just above are photos
of a 'gnu' and a 'goatee.'
In heaven I rule alone
but in the democracy
of the dictionary, I'm one
of many equal neighbors.
And I wonder at this gossamer
system of human signs
which brushes everything catching
nothing but gives me joy
greater than any thing
I ever saw as good.
My hurt is in being all
uncontained, but I step
into the box of this book
and rest, for there I need
not be the Truth but a toy,
the rattle of a word,
radiant and small."

Sunday

God has a mighty, Sunday migraine

Hearing the stridulating chorus
of a million sermons chirped from the pulpit,
he gropes in his breast for mercy, goodness,
like a man who has somehow lost his wallet

While the bells peal through his emptiness
Sunday dongding how they insist
on Sundaying
                this day men address
a faint scrim in the sky, recalling
chaos, abyss, confusion, the warm
plenty of his bosom from which
he plucked them to live on naked earth
going in and out the calendar doors

Inflicting its fragile, ghostly sting,
each "Father in heaven" a hidden rebuke

For Sunday is the day the creation
never rests from metronomic
praise-and-whimper
                  Sunday the world
burst free of him, although he hardly
wanted its birthing and swore he would
never relive the uncontrollable
raw upheaval of self in matter

That Sunday he curled up fetally
like an eternal germ in the ether,
seeing oblivion was good

The Lord's Prayer

Give me this day my daily grain
of some salt detail in the babble of desperate
prayers and praise of my high name,
for I am starved for what they hardly
see — too engrossed in their heavenly dream —
sweetleaf, shadow-play, the grasses . . .
and forgive us our mutual trespasses.

Syndrome

God said, "Doctor, my case is unique,
humanity has broken out
on me like a scarlet rash clouding
my pure transparency, I feel
myself taking on specific location,
precipitating from everywhere,
a focus that makes me dizzy, stress
may be a factor, not since creation
has such a swarm of symptoms attacked.
I am nauseated by men's reverence
and break out in a sweat at the sound of prayer,
I hear the noise of tendons knitting
to bone in me in the dead of night,
I'm being basted and seamed in a body,
and the angels are wise to me, I catch
them with mouths frozen in gaping O's
aghast in the middle of morning praise.
They think the framework of heaven is wormy.
I dream of the sky as a blue womb
with afterbirth of snow and rain,
obsessing that children's play is the only
true religion, because they know
how to build the dazzling white placenta
into a transient man of snow."

Your Honor,

This prisoner is an impostor
claiming to be God-the-Father.
I charge him with impersonating
a ubiquitous deity, receiving
prayers illicitly through psychic
circuits, and molesting the world
while loitering on mountain-peaks.
We seized the prisoner in flagrante
delicto, a peeping Tom of meiosis,
paragenesis, and sundry
low- and high-pressure weather systems.
The perpetrator refused to state
his name and violently resisted
arrest. Instead of the regulation
whites, he was attired in a many-
colored bathrobe. We read him his rights
then asked him to turn out his pockets.
Item: a prurient brochure
on cruises through the human bloodstream
and weekends in the nitrogen cycle.
Item: a mock-up of the solar
system, lasciviously fingered.
Lab analysis reveals
incriminating chlorophyll
clinging to the terrycloth.
And psychiatrists say the evidence strongly
suggests a matter-infatuation
complex due to a weak spiritual
development and lack of lofty
outlets.

What is the prisoner's plea?

31

No Plea

Never mind who I am, I wanted
to get lost out of heaven and haunted
the world for its random situations.
Everything there played to the white
noise of the dice shaken out.
I spent prehistory as the sand
on a beach, religiously shifting, nothing
was more restful than the probable
disposition of every grain.
That was a true vacation, and once
I knew bliss for less than a nanosecond
as the outcome of an atomic collision.
How often I flirted with order, strewing
pebbles in a nearly intelligible
pattern, teasing you into and out
of consummation. Wind was my best
friend and subtle erosion, those restless
gambler's hands. You who are all
form will never understand
the ache of sugar crystals dissolving
or the sacred Koran writing the world
signs and unsigns in ripple and water-
beetle script on tremulous water.

Lethal

God said, "No wonder I am lethal,
I am the war-club man created
to kill the other tribes, but lovely,
too, carved in the living grain and adorned
with the flow of man's own fantasy:
the ancestors thrusting out their tongues,
the constellation of the Hunter,
and the alert script of the Law
all protecting the righteous wielder.
I am the God of the intricate mind
and the mocker of the spilled and bloody
brains, I cannot flee my shape
any more than I can evade my beauty.
As I smash and fall I am bowing down
to the divinity of the hand
that holds the creator in its grip."

Seeing He Was a Museum

In his right hand extended, palm
Upward, he carried a few little faience
Sculptures — hawk, frog, and squatting man.
He wore a gambler's shade above
His eyes and thought it was an awning
Because he was an institution
Rather than a person. He sought
Donations from the Rockefellers
But his carefully worded letters of
Appeal always got filed away.
Undaunted, he petitioned the mayor
For recognition, a blue-ribbon
Ceremony to open him,
And he wanted the council to pass a law
Giving him the absolute right
To commandeer a taxi at any
Time, seeing he was a museum and might
Have to make lightning acquisitions.
He wanted to get to know as many
Men as possible, to travel
Always in a crowd of admirers.
He would have liked the papers to publish
A route of his daily walks so people
Could schedule their visits to him and he wished
To confer with other museums on an equal
Basis, for sometimes, he admitted,
Not everything can be accomplished
With people only, nice as they are.

Also, he wanted to know how the Tate
In London and the Hermitage
In Leningrad were feeling, possibly
Telegrams would serve to extend
Fraternal greetings. And when he decided
To make his Grand Tour, they would be ready
To receive him. Was there a room in museums
Especially set aside for other
Museums when they visited — like Chinese
Boxes nesting inside each other?
What about China, had they abolished
Museums? But mostly he wanted to sense
The crowds streaming out of himself,
Satisfied at closing time.

III

Grandma's Victorian Parlor

Sitting in grandma's Victorian parlor
on the chair with the antimacassar is God,
a green lizard with pulsing throat
and a man's parted, brilliantined hair.
Grandma is serving him crackers, and tea
from a burnished copper samovar.
Everything is as it should be.

"The world is still young, my dear,"
He's telling her, "we must tolerate
medleys, olios, potpourris,
I for one am eternally grateful
to be part of this experiment,
and the service here is excellent,
everything is as it should be."

They're trundling in the guided missiles
to stand by the Maxfield Parrish nudes,
grandma is taking out her Hoover,
while God unfolds his Sunday paper
like a starched shirt dirtied with news:
"Great Victory at Gallipoli —
Everything Is As It Should Be!"

Grandma disguised as Clara Barton
amputates God's noisome tail,
"Be brave, it will soon be over, dear."
But God not missing a jot of his story
regenerates another one —
that crinkled codger is nothing but wounds
and everything is as it should be.

God Contemplates My Grandmother Snoring

in the old-age home, the single hair
on her chin, and since he is God he sees
the troubled medium of her dreams,
which feverishly mingle elders
from shtetls with the Haitian nurses
in a tohu-bohu great as the world's.

And since he is God he cannot tuck
the blanket or fold the sleeves of her sweater,
he cannot even whisk the fly
mizzling across the veined and hilly
parchment-thin skin of her temple.
Such is the helplessness of God!

For he is in a greater extreme
than a ninety-year-old senile woman
confined in a green infirmary.
The fever that wrings him is compassion
and his dream, as clear as hallucination
in every crease and pore, is the world.

"When grandma died in God's dream"

When grandma died in God's dream,
he stirred in his fevered sleep and saw
the sallow ropes pulled hard across
the open grave and knotted to stakes
squatting like toadstools in the dirt;
the mourning sons with contorted mouths;
and the gravediggers stained like the ropes
who shovel earth on the dead for a living
and whose piety is to curse the rain.

When God stirred in grandma's dream,
she saw in her fevered sleep he was stern
with the lineaments of an African king,
the ruler of Songhai or Kanem-Bornu,
and he commanded her to surrender
the ju-ju of senility
for the luminous, boundary-crossing beads
on a bird-mask bordered with cowrie shells,
for the face of her full destiny.

The Kite

The boy constructed a kite and saw
it was good, laths to curve and give
with the wind and tissue-paper strung tight,
a gaudy tail and common twine.
All he wanted was a wind
to lift and bear his bright creation,
air like an animal to poke its muzzle
curiously into the delicious cross.
It floated so high, it was nearly nothing,
except the humming of line when he thrummed,
the tension, yes, that was something
which sang, God was the dot at the end
and the boy could feel that he was good.

Jiggling and antic in the wind,
God looked down from a great height,
a papery two-sided face which saw
everything because it was less
and seemed to plead for its release
speaking in the voice of a boy
laughing and shaken like a toy.

"The hanged teddy bear . . ."

The hanged teddy bear with his red
bow, the tiny llama, the spider
whose web, white patterned on blue,
resembled a snowflake, too pure to fall,
and the housewife-doll exclaiming
"Come in!" at the little portal

were gods singing in the branches, surmounted
by the wilting tinfoil star, their noiseless
song curling through the tinsel, an odorless
vine that cannot choke or breed,
like ladders of silver tears or helplessly
jaunty ribbons whose winks are tics,

the tree a splinter neatly lodged
near the purring, contented radiator,
the tree an array of pert gods,
shrapnel from an ancient explosion,
so many fragments like these lost
in the world and singing a hopeless glory.

In a Barbershop

in heaven they pretend,
although the scissors cut silently, to hear
the small metallic rhythm,
pretend to feel the plastic
combs through their beards and smell
the perfumed powder dabbed
on their necks

in the absolute silence with their eyes
closed they want to believe
in the tiny, indecipherable humming
of the barber — their loftiest meditations
focus on his practiced movements
around the chair

they want everything to occur
in a gentle swirl through the progress
of their haircuts, the radio
station and the jokes and complaints
of old men dimly around them also

and they want in the snippets of conversation
something about the onset of a bitter
winter, something to make it real

Toy Miracles

Who is that small boy kneeling by the stream,
whispering so intimately to water,
that confused multitude, gathering
its jostling force into susceptible
pools, turning transparency into mud
then sculpting that supple earth into sparrows,
twelve of them nearly frightened into flight
by this worker of toy miracles
who claps to release his creatures, "Be gone!"
hurling his iota of dirt
into the vast and astonished sky,
but a playmate comes with a willow-branch, taunting,
scattering the pools that he had entranced.
"Stupid!" — the word like a fleck of spit —
"What did this water do to hurt you?
Now wither and die!" He does. It is Jesus.

IV

Measured Slices

We keep our God confined in the zoo
of heaven, which emits a stench
of straw and feces. Men pass through
in prayer or fantasy and gaze
into the cage where God paces
with a blank look in his eye and murder
shimmering in his stride, or lies
drugged with doses of eternal
time. Even the mockers of impotent power
arrive so clean in this foul place,
ascending through the tops of their heads,
that they are overcome by the odor,
for what is ranker than something feral
clapped in a foursquare space and fed
with measured slices of devotion?

"God has infinite power of change"

God has infinite power of change,
the Proteus of metaphysics,
but not a mite of force to enact
his will in the world; hence he visits
creation as fly, spider, ant,
red-winged blackbird (the epaulets
are thrilling) and so on up the ranks
of animals, showing himself as pest
or threat, but always through a vehicle,
enacting a creature's will not his.
Thus, when God becomes a weed
to approach man from this slant,
he does everything in overabundance,
multiplying helplessly,
declaring war on man's order,
which in his actual self he may
approve, but it's no use, as weed
he greenly overtops our limits.
In this way, we perpetually
are dominating or struggling
against our own deity,
passionate to communicate
with us, of whom he may approve.

On Genesis

Do you think like the worshipping others that God wasn't
   riddled
before Genesis with hateful opposition,
that unstopped mouths didn't cry out of himself,
or wisps of spirit, knotted apparitions
slither in discontent and panic at matter-
to-be, that the fluent Logos wasn't broken
into a manifold chattering appeasement,
the Word begging words for authority
when every incipient shape was in rebellion,
the sequoia in a delirium of debate,
mutinous whispers crowning the nonexistent
trunk, refusing the rightful height and girth
while God was urging the phloem to outlive empires,
and simultaneously he was wheedling
the unborn spirit of the truculent flea
to nurse its grudges in a wingless body;
remember the God that man mirrors was faceless,
so what was there to behold, but this wooing issued
from lipless lips pursuing the stubborn ur-crystals
to inveigle them into a sinewy reptile glitter,
and God played the part of a shameless ventriloquist,
throwing his voice into the dummy void,
which stuttered in tongues of wood like inspired flame,
gurgled and sluiced like runnels, thudded like dirt,
until the reluctant world, seduced by noise,
lurched into being with all its sullen substance.

God Retired

God retired and went to work as a clown,
a little man with a big cigar, strolling
the streets of the city in checked pants, with a cloud
of fleas he called his "adoring angels," a beard,
a tattered jacket. The world was his big top,
the sky his seamless tent they never took down.
He consecrated his life to filling in
the moments of intermission in the traffic,
one of the small mob of cancelled people
clogging and adorning the machinery.
He shoved his hands deep in pockets, blew smoke,
emitted a fine stench, and his office couldn't find
him, all they could say was "retired, gone fishing,"
repeating his note. He was lying near a bank
yelling at two policemen who were climbing out
of their car and putting on heavy gloves to touch him.

Old Man among Old Men

Confess that you are a hopeless voyeur,
flattening your nose to our windows,
loiterer and malingerer,
infecting the air and making it scruffy
and your cheek is a lean and greasy scrag
dabbled with driblets of sweat, confess!
You feed don't you on the sordes
and gurry of our negligent lives,
enjoying a meager ubiquity
in alleyways and by outhouses,
gesticulating like wash on the line
with audacity and quickened color,
O Emperor of All the Mongrels
and Master of Oily Nebulae
smeared across the rain-slicked streets . . .

With the ommatidia of prayer,
I number the hairs on your helplessly breathing
chest, in meditation I tail
you into and out of ramshackle shelters,
in poetry I array you rib
to tibia and phalanges, because
you are more my father than my father,
homeless old man among old men.

Contemporary Prayer

Who is this weakling who is everything,
visible in no particular place
but also the great invalid of space-
time, sprawling everywhere, recuperating,
his tongue lolling amid pulsars and dwarf stars,
his fever evident in the probabilistic
twitching of leptons into and out of creation.

He is our Father, endangered, a species of one,
I nurse and ply him with my midget's whisper
as I swarm over that speck of his body I know,
wheedling and coaxing him with trivia,
while his ears are drummed by exploding supernovae
and everywhere he's distracted by his wambling,
broken symmetries, ill and forgetful.

Father, I pray to you in your sore need,
you who suffer all of matter-energy
and whose dreams expand with the thrust of a fireball
but who cannot lift a pinky to mend the sheath
of a single neuron torn from its groove in muscle.
Father, I feel despair and uncanny pride
as my voice's fingers pluck you out of nothing.

Fragment of a Heretical Testament

At 10^{-43} seconds
into creation God became disabled
by a stroke which separated gravitation
from the strong, weak, and electromagnetic forces
and rendered him an incalculably brooding old man
though without curtailing his phenomenal growth,
particularly that of the divine beard
whose loops and spirals have continued to tickle,
itch, provoke, and scandalize sundry thinkers
and which as we know began to sprout quite early —

At 10^{-6} seconds,
when the universe had cooled sufficiently
for protons to form (God is the only creature
to begin life with senility and then
experience the unbridled growth of a child),
so that some 15×10^9 years later
we are living entangled in that luxuriance
of unclipped whiskers consisting of superclusters
of galaxies, each with $10^{2\,\text{to}\,3}$ clusters, alternating
with spherical or elliptical voids, but imagine

At 10^0 seconds
God's cheekbones, measured now in megaparsecs,
fit in the span of a single centimeter,
a nub or nut from which the hum
of probability ceaselessly issued
(a stunned God and all
that ever was or will be, pulsing
in the palm of your nonexistent hand)
yielding a universe riddled
with insatiable sinkholes and inexhaustible sources.

NOTES

"God's Shame"
    This poem is a complete unit, without a stanza break.

"Seeing He Was a Museum"
    This poem is a complete unit, without a stanza break.

"God Contemplates My Grandmother Snoring"

    shtetls — small Eastern European Jewish
        communities of former times

    tohu-bohu — Hebrew word for chaos

"When grandma died in God's dream"

    ju-ju — A charm or fetish (West Africa)

"Old Man among Old Men"

    The phrase "old man among old men" is a cabalistic
    designation for God.

"Fragment of a Heretical Testament"

    megaparsec — one million times 3¼ light-years